Absent, Present, and Everything Unpleasant

Absent, Present, and Everything Unpleasant

by
Ben Hodgson

Absent, Present, and Everything Unpleasant

First published 2024
001

Text & artworks copyright © Ben Hodgson
Design copyright © Ben Hodgson
Edited by: David Ridd
Cover & interior design: Onur Alka | bookdesign.berlin
Illustrations: Ifrah Fatima

The moral right of the copyright holder has been asserted.

ISBN: 9798320979588 (Paperback)
       9798320981291 (Hardcover)

www.pagesofthemind.com

Disclaimer

The book titled "Absent, Present, and Everything Unpleasant" is intended to provide a personal account of mental health experiences, specifically addressing topics such as depression, suicide, and self-harm. It is important to note that the contents of this book are solely the author's personal experiences and opinions should not be considered professional advice or a substitute for professional guidance.

The author understands that the detailed discussions within this book may be distressing or triggering to certain individuals. It is essential for readers to exercise discretion and self-care when engaging with the content. If you are currently experiencing mental health challenges, it is crucial to prioritise your well-being and consider whether reading this book is appropriate for you at this time.

All content in this book is protected by copyright law. No part of this book may be reproduced, stored in a retrieval system, or transmitted in any form or by any means, electronic, mechanical, photocopying, recording, or otherwise, without the prior written permission of the author.

Contents

Disclaimer

Introduction — 1

The Mind — 6
Empty this space, I want to feel — 8
Dancing with my distractions — 10
Mindful definitions — 11
Illuminating the illusion — 12
"I'm fine" — 14
The quest — 16
A never-ending edge — 18
Trapped thoughts — 19
The unknown — 20
Life's requirements — 22
Beneath the smile — 23
Nature's one true gift — 24
The invitation in your today — 26
Infinite freedom — 28

Struggles in connection — 32
Love, the beginning — 34
An ever-changing landscape — 35
An embrace outside of societal norms — 36
Love's finest display — 38
A hero's predictable demise — 40
A pathway beyond — 41
Building beyond love — 42
The ever-changing shades of love — 44
Easy to spell, difficult to define — 45
Your fragile boundaries — 46
Rebuilding through connection — 47
The duality of loves contrasts — 48
Unseen presence — 49
A warm embrace that has turned cold — 50
The loose definition — 52
Perspective — 53

Eyes of regret	54
Untimed love	56
Two souls, two destinies	57
A fading figure, the loudest goodbye	58
The hidden plot	59
Breaking the cycle	60
Comfort in the depths of loss	62
Mind, body, self-worth	63
Justifying their betrayal	64
Reflection or reaction	66

Unsettled thoughts   70

When simple becomes something bigger	73
Embracing the (im)possible	74
Belittlement of unspoken suffering	76
Beyond belittlement	77
Unwind	78
Rewind	80
A language defined by signs	81
Peace in an anxious mind	82
Finding my freedom	84
The screams in your own silence	86

Processing Grief   90

The absent heart	92
Pouring my love into the circle of life	93
Unseen love	94
Lost without you	96
A scarless soul or a starless night	98
The silence of grief	100
The ever-changing tide	102
Love and grief	104
The echo of lost presence	105
The cracks in our foundations	106
The unspoken cost	108
My family tree	109
Reflection	110
When empathy fails	111
Grieving the unattainable	112

When pain becomes peace	113
The gift between pain and loss	114

Depression   118

Tracing the veins of darkness	120
Unfinished sentences	121
Beyond the label	122
Accepting the past and re-writing the future	123
My inner self-destruction	124
My false promises	126
When memories turn to tears	128
The crushing weight of my insignificance	129
Light will help reunite	130
Harnessing the strength of inner silence	131
It's what helped them...	132
It's what will help you	133
A fragile balance	134
Discovering brightness in fading colours	136
Does time heal wounds?	138
Falling in love with each of life's seasons	139
Waves create a ripple effect	140
Seed to strength	141
Redefining 'I'm fine'	142

The crossroads   146

Present	149
Be a man	150
The crossroads	152
Ending life or ending a life	153
Cultivating kindness in the midst of despair	154
Self-harm makes mental health physical	155
A call for help	156
On the other side	158
Snakes and ladders	159
The curtain that doesn't close	160
When we choose life	162
After and before	163

Ladders and snakes	164
The triangle	166
The circle	167
Lost in my own maze	168

Helping Yesterday's Self — 172

A journey, not a battle	174
Whispered opportunities	175
Alone but empowered	176
Rethinking inner fulfilment	178
Light in her tears	179
Immeasurable	180
Depression	182
Drive or destroy	183
Time	184
The weight of unresolved pain	186
Rediscovery around what matters	187
Behaviours and the heart	188
The line between love and loss	189
The coffee shop	190
In my silence	191

The Road Ahead — 194

Meet the Author — 198

A heartfelt thank you	202

Dear Pain,

I wrote a letter to you
that was never sent.

It helped me process the past and
embrace the present.

It said,
I understand,
and the things I don't understand,
I accept....

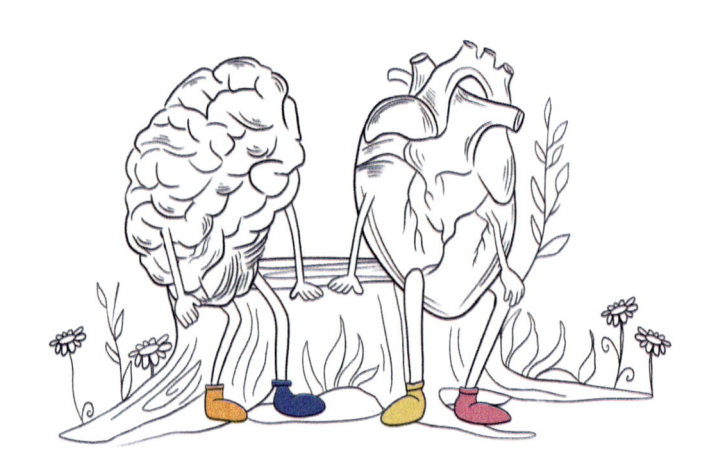

Introduction

Two years ago, I stood at a crossroads. Directionless, constantly depressed, and filled with never-ending grief, anxiety, and pain. It was inescapable. Every day, I stood there, unable to see past my suffering. Every day, I wished the choice of life or death would disappear entirely. During these moments, I wanted to sink beneath the road, desperately hoping that if I could remove the path ahead, I could permanently end the grief, the anxiety, and the pain.

I wanted to die. Plain and simple. I wanted the out.

I wrote on the notes section of my phone. "*I want this life to end. I want to escape the pain*". It was an emotionless thought, something so final that felt so natural. Something happened when I wrote that – this sudden feeling of relief – this quietening of the voice inside my head. So, I wrote more.

In the earlier stages of my writing, I was transported back to one of my earliest childhood memories. A moment in a vast forest where I created my own trail, showcasing my curious nature whilst also highlighting my utter lack of navigational prowess – a trait that I still struggle with to this day.

My daring adventure did not consider the hours of anxious searching my family would have to undertake when they realised I had slipped away from their protective gaze. But to everyone's surprise, when they did finally find me, I was happily perched atop a tree stump singing to myself merely.

The significance of this memory is how powerful pausing can be; simply observing the world around us and spending time with our thoughts can be a beautiful thing.

I find myself revisiting this memory often, placing myself on that tree stump once again with a want to find answers. To my emotions, my feelings, and my behaviours. Answers to *why* I was the way I was. There wasn't a goal in mind when I started. It wasn't to write a book, a poem, or even a hastily scribbled note on my phone. The goal was to understand the maze. To review the journey that had landed me here.

In writing, I stopped looking for the next road to take. I settled myself right in the centre of the crossroads and wrote about what might be – what was behind me – and why the option to end things felt so appealing in the first place.

My journalling transformed into an intense journey of introspection and self-discovery. Writing was a way to express my emotions and allowed me to note down everything I felt – whenever the feelings came. I became the wallflower observing the thoughts in my head. Examining emotions, how they acted, and what encouraged them to stay. Writing peeled back each layer of the onion, and sure, it brought tears, but through those, I gained a deeper understanding of myself.

To my surprise, poetry occupied most of my writing. I say "surprise", as in school, I was always disinterested in their melodic rhythm and deeper meanings. However, recently, I have begun to understand the profound depth that existed in the words laid out on the page. It felt like a golden ticket to discovering a new way to explore my innermost thoughts and feelings. It was a safe space. A quiet corner in my head that I became fond of visiting.

In these pages, I offer that poetry. I offer the words I wrote to my past self and share all the feelings, thoughts, and insights that helped me heal and return to myself. Don't worry; this isn't a complicated book filled with theories and psychological jargon. It's as raw and real as the journal at my bedside.

The Mind

For most of my life, my mind felt like a confusing space. Somewhere inside that space, the person I was or might become floated about. I searched for landmarks, consistency – something to hold on to. But the intricacies of the mind felt so complex and distant that I felt like an intruder within. Something out of place in a weird void that could neither be tamed nor controlled.

My internal monologue was my constant companion. During my mental health struggles, it criticised my every move and reinforced my every worry. Escaping this relentless cycle was challenging, and I came to view this inner voice as my adversary. However, this mindset did not bring me any closer to peace; instead, it pushed me further from my authentic self. On better days, I found inspiration in the messages of encouragement, praise, and wisdom that my inner dialogue occasionally provided. Yet, the stark contrast between these positive moments and the negative ones on difficult days intensified my struggles.

My exploration began by making small, microscopic decisions and seeing where I could plant my feet. Where I had steady, or at least, less shaky ground. The question is: *how do you start that exploration of the mind?*

For myself, therapy was the first step – a way to explore my behaviours, as well as my conscious and unconscious feelings and thoughts. I knew my mind was manipulating the space around me, so I became the explorer of *why*. This saw me looking at my beliefs, desires, and passions. Uncovering the intricacies behind my existence and how these defined my being.

Alongside therapy, my journaling practice helped me develop a more balanced relationship with my inner voice. I assumed the role of an observer, watching my thoughts without attempting to control them. This perspective allowed me to see my thoughts for what they truly were. Giving me space to reflect and gently come to resolutions.

As I began to heal, I was able to better understand myself and how to best look after my mental health and wellbeing. After spending so long at the crossroads, it felt incredibly empowering to be making so many positive changes for myself. A crucial turning point for me was rediscovering that kindness originates from within. Learning how to be kind and compassionate to myself was such an important part of my journey. Like with everything in life, it was a skill which I had to practice, and it wasn't always straightforward. Ironically, these challenges presented even more chances for me to hone these qualities through practice!

Kindness also had a profound impact on my relationships. I didn't tear myself or others down; instead, I wanted to lift them up, support them, and help them succeed in their own journeys. Gone are the feelings of jealousy and resentment towards those taking different and exciting paths. In their place, I now experience excitement and compassion, eager to see those I love and care about doing well.

Cultivating a more positive relationship with my mind has been an extraordinary journey. The poetry I composed during this period played a significant role in enabling me to delve into and articulate my emotions and insights from this transformative experience. My focus was exploration, finding landmarks in my mind, and trying to determine what made each tick. What were the triggering points of the inner critic and anxiety that wouldn't quit?

Empty this space, I want to feel

Busy, lost,
confused

Is this how this
space is used?

Quiet, grounded,
and precise

A place called
home

A place for
advice

A space to nurture
and adore

Where you are
your own captain

As you begin
to explore

Dancing with my distractions

This place offered me
the past and the present

With sadness and regret,
this space became unpleasant

It created all these feelings
and reactions

My mind focused on each
tempting distraction

I'd dance around the truth
that was felt within

Learning that without facing
this, true recovery could not begin

The mind was lazy
and protective

Shielding me from the agonising
pain was the objective

Destruction became my home
and all that remained was the unknown

Mindful definitions

A smashed mirror
shows an imperfect
reflection

However,

It is not the mirror
that decides worth in
this broken projection

Illuminating the illusion

A beginning
and an end

Is it your foe
or is it your friend?

A battle that we were
never taught to embrace

Do we really know how
to conquer this inner space

The patterns can
start to appear

Your mind spirals
and is filled with fear

In these moments,
have you tried to find the light

Reflecting is one way
to make sure it shines bright

"I'm fine"

6 letters, two words,
a clear sign

Easy to spell,
but so difficult to define

Although I have these
two words by my side

My mind is trapped, and
happiness isn't something it can provide

I say these words to
support my denial

And most of the time
it's a fractured smile

So, here's to my 6 letters,
my two words, my clear sign

Hide the pain,
and tell the world 'I'm fine'...

The quest

The mind creates
expectation

It controls our reaction
to every situation

Do we spend life
chasing this illusive thing

Wondering whether we will
achieve the happiness it should bring

When we question what
we are truly searching for

We realise we have had this
feeling once or twice before

Once I have this or that,
I will feel complete

The underlying sadness
this brings is so discreet

In time, you realise it's
important to be realistic with goals

It's one of the few things
we can truly control

A never-ending edge

A continued shape. No sides or breaks and no escapes. A never-ending curve. No right angle to sit on and observe. No perspectives or shadows where we can hide. A never-ending curve. No right angle to sit on and observe. No corners or shapes where we can hide. An infinite space to explore. When you look at it from the outside, the round sides represent new perspectives of your creativeness. You see this shape can be two things. A place of kindness and peace. Where did your mind explore this? Those associations are yours to agree or dismiss. A place to explore. Where the round sides of your mind increase. How your thoughts begin. An infinite space to explore. A place of kindness and peace. A continuous barrier on the inside.

18

Trapped thoughts

Our minds can get stuck
Falling into a mental block or rut

When we take a bird's eye view
We can then look down on ourselves and review

Contrast can make our today feel so plain
When we compare, remember no two lives are the same

The next chapter is so close
As contrast will make you appreciate this change the most

It's not a bad life, it's a bad day
Sometimes it's hard to keep our spiralling minds at bay

Remember to reflect on what your dream life used to be
You're living that, but I know it's sometimes hard to see

The unknown

Being in our own company is a unique thing
How do we describe the emotions this brings?

When alone, we often look to the future or the past
Do we ever think presently and want this moment to last?

Try sitting alone with your beautiful mind
And allow the use of this time to remain undefined

Let the voice in your head be gentle with you
Take in your environment and take a bird's eye view

Observe yourself from above
Remembering self-care starts with love

This was just a few words about enjoying time alone
Your mind is its own artist, an explorer of the unknown

> In time, joy will fill the part of us that was once filled with silence

Life's requirements

The perfect mind
The perfect body

The perfect house
The perfect partner

The perfect outfit
The perfect life

Which of the above can we really sustain?
As upholding this image can leave us drained

If these things are the identity of what we could be
How much of our present world is left to see?

We should accept the imperfections in our life today
As each day passes, it gives us lessons along the way

Beneath the smile

Struggles can be hidden by a smile
So, check in on that happy friend every once in a while

The simple act of asking someone if they are ok
Can be enough to brighten their day

We are conditioned to answer *not bad, thank you*
Even when we are struggling to see this life through

The mind is such a complicated place
And it can spiral at an alarming pace

There is strength in making change
Even if being vulnerable may feel a little strange

So, I say you are truly enough as you are,
the journey may have just started,
but you have already got this far...

Nature's one true gift

So much happiness can
be found in nature

Let your mind daydream
and become your own creator

Take in the simple
patterns of the clouds

Listen to the world's symphonies
and all the other beautiful sounds

For you will find joy in our
greatest playground

Where sadness can be lost,
and serenity found

Pause, take a moment for
yourself and how you feel

Live presently and embrace
the beauty the world has revealed

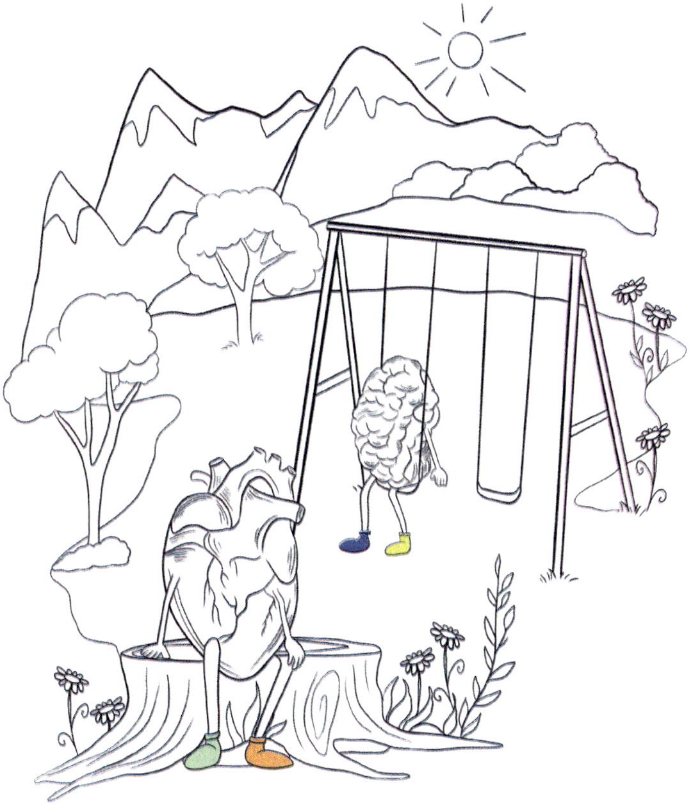

The invitation in your today

It takes courage to
change your today

Needing consistent
effort along the way

Live boldly and honestly,
I know you can

Life doesn't follow one single,
rigid plan

What is it that you
are waiting for?

You've hit bumps in
the road once or twice before

You do not need
answers to every question

Living presently is a positive
and life-changing suggestion

You can never imagine the
extent of what's ahead in every direction

Deal with your today and
work on that mind and body connection

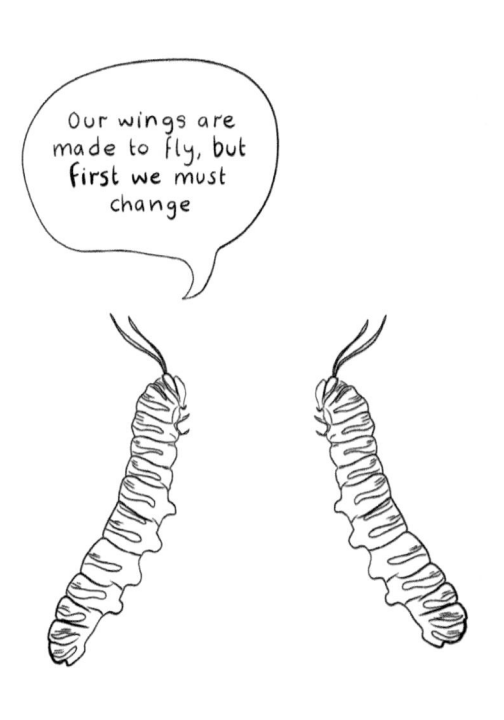

"Our wings are made to fly, but **first** we must change"

Infinite freedom

Bound by nothing
but your mind

A realm to explore,
a secret to find

This is a new chapter
in your storyline

You're happy alone,
surely this is a sign

A sign to live as the most
authentic version of you

Embracing who you are,
and not letting distractions obstruct the view

Struggles in connection

Within anxiety and depression existed a steep uphill battle that challenged the very core of my ability to connect with others. Amidst this internal struggle, a feeling of distance stayed with me, making it harder to bridge the gap between my emotional landscape and the outside world. Questions echoed in my mind, yet these questions, as important as they were, remained unanswered. Causing a disconnect that challenged my core throughout much of my adult life.

Avoidance was often my most successful coping mechanism, a respite from my inner turmoil. It wasn't until I arrived at the crossroads that I truly searched for answers. To fully engage with life, I had to answer many of the questions that existed within the most painful parts of my mind. In these questions, I sought benchmarks—examples that showed the extent of my distance from the world that surrounded me.

Reflecting on my experiences with romantic love and relationships was an important part of my recovery. I was able to recognise many deep-rooted insecurities that had played out on repeat in previous connections. One of the most intense emotions was an overpowering sense of unworthiness. I felt a persistent uncertainty about whether I deserved the person sitting before me. The problem was that my thoughts and feelings were not grounded in reality and instead were fuelled by my constant negative inner dialogue. Often, I would find myself placing them on a pedestal, elevating them to an unrealistic standard that caused an unhealthy imbalance in the relationship dynamics. In doing so, I inadvertently expected them to fulfil all my emotional needs. It wasn't until I recognised this unconscious behaviour that I could trace it back to its root cause: a profound lack of self-kindness and self-compassion.

After reflecting on my challenges with self-compassion, I came to realise the extent of how it was affecting me. I found it difficult to trust or recognise genuine expressions of love from others. Even in moments when love was generously offered, my heart resembled a broken glass. As quickly as love was given, it vanished, seeping through the cracks, and leaving me yearning for more attention and affection. The persistent need for more love was a constant reminder of the fragility of my connection with myself. In my story, it was never about the absence of love shown to me, but more so, it was about my ability to let myself really experience and embrace it. At the crossroads, a moment of profound honesty revealed that perhaps my learned behaviours were not only unproductive but also limiting, especially in the context of forming connections with others.

Like the majority of young people today, I considered social media a vital tool for creating and maintaining connections. However, I also experienced numerous challenges and issues associated with social media use. During my recovery, I began to recognise that social media fuelled many of my insecurities. It had shaped a somewhat warped idea of what a relationship should be. I found myself constantly bombarded with seemingly perfect examples as people shared only the best of what they were experiencing. But instead of being influenced by unrealistic standards set by social media, I took time to reflect on my values and what genuinely brings me fulfilment and happiness. I realised that love should harmonise with my beliefs and aspirations, creating an ongoing journey rather than fixating on a final destination. By connecting with my own journey, it became easier to navigate the complexities of modern relationships and I was then able to foster connections that resonated with my authentic self.

This introspective process was highly personal. Where what mattered most was what made me feel loved, valued and seen for who I truly was. At the core of this reflection was honouring my connection with self, which then shaped the pathway for some beautiful platonic relationships on this journey.

In this passage sit some beautiful conversations with those around me, who, in my time of learning, shared many of their lessons and advice on the theme of love and connection. In searching for answers, I was determined not to let my experiences limit my understanding in an area that one day will shape a significant part of my life.

Over time, I have learned to romanticise my moments of solitude, finding beauty and fulfilment in the quiet companionship I have with myself. And whilst my heart remains open to romantic love, I am enjoying this period of self-discovery. Observing the world in my bonus years has undeniably been a beautiful experience.

Love, the beginning

Love begins with focusing
on your own journey

Don't let society determine
whether you're late or early

Ultimately, there is only
one you

Looking internally is the
only fair way to review

Society may dictate
this or that

Celebrate differences as
this is where true happiness is at

It's important in this life
to allow for mistakes

Doing something wrong
should never be, make or break

They call life a lesson,
but it's only a lesson if you learn

Be kind to yourself,
As this will allow your mind to give you love in return

An ever-changing landscape

Oh, how complex
they can be

A whole world that
only you and I see

We hoped that under the
surface something deeper exists

Is our lack of commitment
something we all miss?

The landscape
has changed

I see constants highlight reels
and don't think it's strange

Have these highlights
given false representation of what they are

The stages of connection, distorted,
almost bizarre

An embrace outside of societal norms

Some believe length and strength
go hand in hand

Marriage after a set amount of
years is assumed to be planned

When did society give us
deadlines for these moments

Love without these things is
seen as a missing component

Yet true love lies in celebrating
each and every day

Remembering all the special
moments along the way

So don't give in to the outside
pressures society brings

Accepting your partners
quirks is where true love begins

Love's finest display

A fire burned
in my heart

A feeling,
a yearning for this chapter to start

For in these moments,
I feel alone

Where loves most
authentic form is shown

True, perfect,
and seemingly attainable

A lifelong promise,
something so sustainable

But love is never
defined by a day or a ring

It's a complex,
multi-layered thing

Easy to spell,
but hard to define

Tell the world I'm ok without it,
I'm doing just fine...

A hero's predictable demise

It's difficult to show you
what you can't see

Happy and strong alone
is something you should be

You can't ever force
someone to care for you

What would happen if their
love was something they withdrew?

Would you be something
that was truly missed

Or another failed talking
stage that is dismissed

It asks, why do we always
want to fix what is unfixable

You want to be the hero,
but the ending is predictable

An ending that
turns into a pattern

You act surprised when
you knew this would happen...

A pathway beyond

Intimacy and vulnerability
go hand in hand

When you face pain alone,
it's harder to understand

Intimacy can be bigger
than something sexual

When did you last discuss
something intellectual?

Take a moment to speak openly
with your significant other

When you listen intently,
there is so much to discover

Discovery is such a
fantastic thing

And is where the journey
with vulnerability begins

Building beyond love

It's hard to accept that
love is not enough

Simply loving more will
make this partnership more tough

You need to understand
their perspectives

Otherwise working
together is ineffective

Shared values are the key
to achieving something higher than love

Please put trust in what I
have written in the above

It will help you build something
more than just you two

Distinguish love from lust,
don't get them misconstrued

The ever-changing shades of love

A simple word,
a choice

When spoken aloud, it
finds its powerful voice

It is easy to love in the
bright moments

Marriage, a home,
all the special components

What shape does
this word take

When I am hurting and
have made another mistake

I may enter a period of
darkness and pain

When no light shines within,
do you still love me the same?

Easy to spell, difficult to define

What do we call love
without its name

A four-letter word,
a devastating game

We run from it,
trying to switch lanes

Pretending the path
isn't destruction or pain

Escaping ownership,
but embracing blame

After all, language
gives it a title, a simple name

Your fragile boundaries

When we talk about the
value that they bring

Do we consider where
the painful cost begins

The more chances
that you give

Increases the number
of times you have to forgive

When they see a pattern
of forgiveness

It's a sign that they
can start to give less

They know the answer
no matter what

With every conversation
ending with *if*, *what*, and *but*

Rebuilding through connection

Abandonment in your
past can be detected

You see rejection as
something that's expected

These patterns show
the hurt that's yet to heal

Influencing your emotions
and everything you feel

When you argue,
are you the first to give an out?

Your fear of abandonment
is what this is about

Exploring and discussing
problems is a powerful thing

Don't jump to conclusions and
allow the work to begin

The work towards unlearning
this particular reaction

Will help avoid every
argument ending in dissatisfaction

The duality of loves contrasts

To feel love,
is to feel pain

Impossible to define,
difficult to explain

Love can be such a
beautiful thing

But with loss,
pain is what love brings

Forever entwined

When we find one,
the other isn't far behind

Unseen presence

I mean a little to a lot,
and a lot to a few

I am just a shadow,

From someone you loved,
to someone you outgrew

A warm embrace that has turned cold

For the world
still goes round

and the pages
still turn

But what is a life
without a love

that will never return

The loose definition

Sometimes
you love

And sometimes
you give

Sometimes you have
to deal with silence

And sometimes you
have to learn to forgive

Sometimes
you hurt

And sometimes
it ends in pain

And sometimes the
definition of love,

will never feel the same again

Perspective

In English, we say
"*love*"

In poetry, we say

"*Love is pain,
two four-letter words
with different spellings,
but the same name*"

Eyes of regret

Love and art sat behind
those deep brown eyes

Telling a story as beautiful
as my first sunrise

How could a
simple gaze

Say so many different things,
in so many different ways

Pain, passion,
and everything in-between

But I never
asked the question

So, we remained as a
what could've been

Untimed love

The distance between
the earth and moon

Where our lives collided
a little too soon

We were always meant to
be together

But it ended before we
could see our forever

A star that didn't belong
in each other's night sky

Where the most painful
word was our final *goodbye*

Two souls, two destinies

We were forever
and a day

A connection that said
all the words we wanted to say

Home was **found** in each
other from the start

The love blinded our
minds and filled our hearts

It is **peace**ful that our
future is so known

I'd never want to travel
this world alone

Time stopped when
we were together

And time **apart**
felt like forever

A fading figure, the loudest goodbye

Sometimes love
alone is enough

It's important to **love**
more when times get tough

It **is** an act,
not a service

A word that holds
one particular purpose

A word that gives us
something to believe in

Something that ties us together
and stops the other from **leaving,**

sometimes a word that
is difficult to define

love, the one consistency
in our timeline

In the darkness
and the light

Our love **is** what continues
to shine bright

I could never process the
thought of **letting** you **go**

A life without your presence,
is something I never want to know

The hidden plot

When the words love
and story come together

People think it starts now,
and lasts forever

But the word story suggests
it has already been told

A warm embrace that has
now turned cold

When we call it
love alone

This is a presence,
not an unknown

And when it is a love that
never begins

This is imagination,
a storyline where no one wins

Maybe the only
love is known within

And it's a path to be explored,
not something to lose or win

Breaking the cycle

To avoid patterns, it's crucial to process the past
Being self-aware ensures a relationship will last

If you can look at yourself and find the things you want to adjust
It will prevent you from going for the next person in lust

Take your time when you want to find your next human
As unresolved trauma could consume them

People often think there is weakness in being alone
Outside opinions don't matter, as this is your life to own

It is better to stand on your own two feet
Rather than finding someone else to make you feel complete

If you search for a quick fix
Your ability to process your emotions will end in conflict

Your person is around the corner, my friend
This is just a poem to explain why I want this cycle to end

Comfort in the depths of loss

I'm proud we let each other go,
as this started the journey for me to grow

For a few months, I was scared special couldn't happen twice,
as I felt lonely in those winter nights

But life always comes together in a weird way,
the special I found was being me in the today

The expectation was that we would always be together,
I realise now it's important to focus on the today and not the forever

Relationships are incredibly complex things,
as we never know what life brings

We find comfort in the people we love deeply,
and sometimes, we lose ourselves completely

To love deeply, you must love yourself first,
otherwise, the love you give out seems a little rehearsed

I have no regret in the past,
but sometimes, love alone is not enough for a relationship to last...

Mind, body, self-worth

Those who are
meant for us, stay

Those who aren't,
will teach you important lessons along the way

Sometimes things
won't work out

And sometimes,
doubt may linger about

How about if the rejection
has provided redirection?

Helping you realise life can
never be this fairy tale of perfection

Relationships are such
complex things

Being truly vulnerable with
each other is where this journey begins

Just remember your worth is
not determined by the words of others

Worth is determined by what
your mind and body think of one another

Justifying their betrayal

When you ask
should I be here

Is being alone again
the thing, you fear?

When you justify the
behaviour of that person

Your ability to protect
your boundaries will worsen

When we are happy
and content in the today

We don't question whether
this person should stay

Often questions can be a
sign of where expectations are not met

Each time behaviours repeat
themselves, you seem to forget

Forgetting that we have been
here once or twice before

Which should remind you,
that this is what boundaries are for…

Reflection or reaction

If someone arrives and gives
what you cannot provide

Will you choose anger or reflection,
only one can be your guide

When someone so
quickly takes your place

Anger and confusion can
become your safe space

How can love be turned
off so fast

Remember love like this
isn't here to last

It's important to remember
we heal at different rates

Our journey is within and
only something we can create

So, focus on yourself as you
both begin new lives

Finding yourself rather than
finding someone else is where you will thrive

Unsettled thoughts

Anxiety was like a dark cloud that followed me everywhere I went, hovering above my head and casting a shadow over my thoughts. It was a constant companion that never let me forget my insecurities, fears, and doubts. I thought I was being proactive by anticipating every possible outcome, but I was drowning in my worries.

Looking back, I can see how my mind worked like a tangled web of insecurities and neediness. Reassurance became my crutch. My constant ally in an unpredictable and frightening world. I constantly sought it from those around me, desperate for someone to tell me everything would be okay. But no matter how many kind words I heard, it was never enough. The anxiety continued to grip me in its suffocating embrace, squeezing tighter and tighter with each passing day.

The reality was that I was caught in a vicious cycle of self-doubt and fear, with every thought adding to an ever-increasing emotional burden. Being genuinely present was not a skill I could master, with an all-consuming focus on what was coming next. My mind could not find safety in the unknown, and the perceived safety blinded me to thoughts anxiety gave me.

I enforced a rigid structure in my life to cope with my anxiety. Everything was planned, including my approach to specific situations and potential outcomes. The thought of embracing the moment or living in the present was too overwhelming for me. I began obsessively planning the following year and the next five years and how this would perfectly fit the timeline of society's expectations. Milestones like marriage, a home and children were already set in stone, regardless of the future challenges.

With my battles, anxiety played a big part in my inability to speak out. The fear was all-consuming, trapping me in a cycle I felt I could never escape. My mind was busy with worries, and I lacked the strength and courage to speak my truth. As a man, I fit the mould quite well. Almost 6ft, an avid gym goer, a rugby player, a respectable job. But beneath the surface sat a profound contradiction, almost like a tightrope, where one wrong step would see this perfect balancing act come tumbling down. In my perceived strength on the outside was a deep fragility that existed. My inner child cowering in the corner, scared of showing any vulnerability to the world. My strength felt fraudulent in a way, an image of contradictions. Outwardly, I would present an unwavering smile. Yet within was a deep absence of feeling, a constant cloud that seemed to follow my every step.

I felt weak for struggling and too ashamed to make that first step. But I have come to know that true strength lies in facing challenges head-on and working towards a healthier and happier self. The power of acceptance became a game-changer for me. By genuinely embracing my behaviours and thoughts, I could better understand my anxiety.

This newfound understanding and perspective allowed me to start progressing towards recovery and healing. My fascination with the mind continued and witnessing my own transformations served as a powerful motivator. The voice in my head was pivotal in my worries, anxious behaviours and even panic attacks. It's as if it became the narrator for my innermost fears, guiding me down paths untravelled. But through acceptance and understanding, I realised I could change the narrative within – a story unfolded, filled with peace, self-love and a newfound sense of hope.

The story saw me exploring how my mind had unconsciously adopted certain behaviours. I became acutely aware of areas where I needed to re-educate myself to unravel old patterns and replace them with new, healthier ones. Throughout this learning journey, I often compared how I spoke to others and how I spoke to myself. This simple question reminded me of the kindness I could show others and encouraged me to extend that compassion to myself. My therapist once shared with me some advice that always stays at the forefront of my mind: *speak to yourself as though you're comforting a child*. Often, the reassuring and soft words became a place of comfort for me.

Initially, I held the belief that avoiding the pain would shield me from further hurt. However, I came to realise that, in reality, confronting the triggers became the source of many answers. Every time a trigger surfaced, it highlighted something I had yet to fully process or find peace with. Though challenging, this process proved to be a rewarding and enlightening way to delve into my unconscious and decipher previously unexplainable behaviours.

I have realised that life is full of uncertainties, many entirely out of my control. But by embracing the unknown, I have removed the structure around my thoughts and the reassurance I used to get from spiralling. As time passed, I began to question my thoughts more and whether they truly aligned with my values and beliefs. Within this journey sat challenges and conversations, which I explore further in this chapter.

When simple becomes something bigger

Anxiety can
come in waves

Choosing how our body
in social situations behaves

It cannot find safety
in the unknown

As the safe space can
only be found when I'm alone

When it is me,
myself, and I

I don't have to tense
up when I reply

You see new people
can cause concern

They flood my view
and anxious thoughts return

Some are not aware of
the trouble's anxiety can trigger

A basic interaction can become
something so much bigger

Embracing the (im)possible

Anxiety

Something so loud,
that whispered so quietly

At the mercy of
everything it had to say

Clouding my happiness,
day after day

The label became
part of me

Stopping me from becoming
the person I wanted to be

I learnt to let go of what
I couldn't control

Only worrying about the things,
I could, was the goal

So, here's to connecting
my mind, body, and heart

Welcoming my new inner dialogue,
a bright new start

Belittlement of unspoken suffering

Calm down

But I can't, my thoughts
feel like I'm going to drown

It's all in your head

Where do you suggest
I put these thoughts instead?

It's really not a big deal

How dare you belittle
something I feel

Everything will be fine

Doesn't the weight of my
worries give you a sign?

Other people have it worse

Struggles are personal it's not
like some consistent curse

Just use your logic

The pain isn't just mental,
it's chronic

Beyond belittlement

*But I can't, my thoughts
feel like I'm going to drown*

Don't pressure yourself,
answers don't have to be found

*Where do you suggest I
put these thoughts instead?*

Embrace the moment and
give yourself time for your head

*How dare you belittle
something I feel*

You don't have to have
answers right away for this ordeal

*Doesn't the weight of my
worries give you a sign?*

Processing your worries
will help you along the line

Unwind

*Is it being truthful
about a situation?*

Or has your anxious mind
turned something small into a full evaluation?

*Is it giving you a genuine
reason not to go?*

Or has your anxious mind
become incredibly scared of the unknown?

*Is it giving a reasonable reaction
to the hand you've been dealt?*

Or is your anxious mind cycling
through the painful emotions you've felt?

*Is it giving you reason to
be scared?*

Or is your anxious mind telling
you silence means no one cares?

Rewind

*Has your anxious mind turned
something small into a full evaluation?*

Reassure yourself and
re-evaluate the situation

*Has your anxious mind become
incredibly scared of the unknown?*

Please speak out,
I promise you are not alone

*Is your anxious mind cycling
through the painful emotions you've felt?*

Review your past and understand
the hand you've been dealt

*Is your anxious mind telling you
silence means no one cares*

When it comes to your struggles,
I promise they are not unaware

A language defined by signs

The anxious mind
Excessive worrying is a normal part of my being

The anxious mind
Excessive worrying means I can't see the world everyone else is seeing

The anxious mind
Restlessness is a feeling that has become my home

The anxious mind
Restlessness is an emotion that makes me feel so alone

The anxious mind
Tiredness consumes my entire self

The anxious mind
Tiredness places happiness on an unreachable shelf

The anxious mind
When it has this label, do words become harder to find?

When we repeat something 7 times
Do we start to understand all of the signs?

The signs that this is something that is part of you
Understanding the symptoms will help see this through

Peace in an anxious mind

Happiness remains
as an elusive being

Every outcome is
something I was seeing

The exploration of
each situation

Had a consistent
association

An association that the
outcome will be a negative one

These relentless thoughts are not
something I could ever outrun

Why, when exploring every outcome,
do we not look for light

It's like our minds are conditioned
not to see anything that shines bright

You hear, calm down it's
all in your head

Everything is fine,
think of something different instead

How is that possible when
our minds are so conditioned to be this way

I know people are trying to help
and say the words I want them to say

But do they understand how hard it is
to live with an anxious mind, day by day

Finding my freedom

An end to this
part of my being
and how it shaped
the world I was seeing

Structured and
without compromise,
my constant spiralling
left nothing as a surprise

This version of me wasn't
something I realised I'd become,
I understand now that the
past cannot be undone

Unchangeable by nature,
the past paves the way,
for something much greater,
a brighter new day

I have found freedom in
letting the river of life flow
and remain comfortable
with the unknown

Tomorrow now appears as a gift
And I live presently, as otherwise
treasure in the present moment
will be missed

The screams in your own silence

Your bed is no longer
a place of rest,
your body has relaxed,
but your mind is being put to the test

It's the moments when you
are truly alone,
spiralling thoughts are what
makes this room feel like home

Home in the way you are
familiar with the headspace you are in,
the silence eats away at you,
and the evaluation begins

The mind focuses on
everything but the present,
your being is acting as some
kind of depressant

It's important to remember
that life isn't one big masterplan,
thinking freely without structure,
was where my journey began

Processing Grief

The death of my mother during childhood left a void and empty space in my heart that felt like a constant presence in my life. As I grew up and reached life's milestones, I couldn't shake the feeling that something was missing. Each landmark and each achievement felt hollow without her presence.

This left a shadow, a grief that I felt I had to endure. A force that kept me from moving forward and progressing in life. The reality of my grief was a profound yearning for my mother. However, having lost her at such a young age, my memory of her transformed into a creation of my own mind – a vision shaped by my perceptions of who or what I thought a mother should be. In my darkest hours, I berated myself for what I had become and for not being what I thought she would want me to be. The haunting question of *'Have I made her proud?'* followed me everywhere. Her absence was completely overwhelming at times, and it took me a long while to realise I was punishing myself over something I had no control over.

It wasn't until I reached my lowest point that I understood my need to relearn and re-evaluate everything I knew about grief. Everything I had been told or observed. Everything I had imagined in my mind. I deconstructed all the preconceived notions, external influences, and internalised images that had shaped my understanding. Confronting the true essence of grief and acknowledging its profound impact on me became a painful yet necessary and introspective journey—one for which I am genuinely grateful.

Grief, for me, does not have an end nor a beginning - it is something we carry throughout life, a loss ever-present in our minds. Sometimes, a piece of us can feel lost forever, taking the memories, laughter, and love with it. The intertwinement of love and grief is fascinating, as having one without the other is rare. With time, I have come to understand the complexities of this journey. Reflecting on my story, as well as others', has offered meaning to the intricate emotions involved, which served as a guide on how to navigate the path forward.

For much of my life, I understood grief to only be linked to death, a permanent loss. Yet upon reflection, I've come to realise grief is a far-reaching emotion capable of encompassing a multitude of experiences beyond mortality. It extends its grasp to various forms of loss, be it the end of a relationship, the closure of a chapter in life, the departure from a familiar place, or the relinquishing of an identity once held dear. It is an emotion that changes us, leaving a mark on our hearts and souls that will always remain. A fundamental part of the human experience which works in diverse and unexpected ways.

Life is full of complexities, and relationships and friendships, like winding paths, can shift unexpectedly, leaving us with a loss that is hard to comprehend. The pain stems from the imagined future you had hoped to share with them. The plans, dreams and shared aspirations. The loss is not as simple as two people going in different directions. It is so much greater than that. In these moments, it's important to reflect and consciously process the loss. As without proper reflection, we hide and overlook the potential for growth and the valuable lessons from this period.

Grief is a multi-layered and complex thing that often extends past just the person's physicality. We often grieve for the person and the future we feel we could have had. I learnt to find reassurance in the memories I did have and not the ones I could have. And only by truly embracing the known when it came to loss did I start to truly heal.

Within this healing was an acceptance that grief can rarely be accurately described in just words alone. My poetry almost served as a guide for my thoughts as they passed through my mind. Simplifying something that, in the past, seemed so deeply complex.

The absent heart

The feeling
comes and goes

As we experience higher
highs and lower lows

A chapter about
this five-letter word

Where the line between
depression and sadness become blurred

It can be so hard
to understand

As you live life
without their guiding hand

Loss can be experienced
in so many ways

Wearing masks,
that present a new identity each day

Pouring my love into the circle of life

The shadow of your
former self is clear to see

I didn't realise grief could
hit me to this degree

A silhouette of
yesterday's self

Reminding us that the circle
of life starts with health

Is the contrast a
negative thing

Or is it a positive reminder of
all the happiness you used to bring

We shared and continue
to share the gift that is today

You have helped shape my
life and taught me many lessons along the way

You may feel like
you have less to give

But as the circle comes to a close,
it's our turn to give you everything we can give

Unseen love

It's hard to put a definition
on what a mum should be

The pain of losing my own
was hard to see

For my entire life, I wondered
what it would be like

To be held in your arms
and told goodnight

With help, I have been able
to process this loss

Your name has become
so much more than what's written on your cross

There are people in my life
who love me like you would

They have helped me see the
light and made sure my thoughts were understood

They supported me when my
world felt like it was ending

And made me realise my time
on this earth was worth extending

Although my recovery
was of my doing

They were there showing me
love when suicidal thoughts were brewing

Lost without you

A symphony
with no conductor

A ship with no
anchor

A compass with
no needle

A film with no
director

The music was a dull drone
And the ship was lost, with nowhere to call home

The compass didn't know where it would land
And the film had no storyline planned

To Mum, Mummy and mother
We may not have properly met in this world
But we may meet in another...

A scarless soul or a starless night

To see
the night,

but to ignore
the stars

Is to see
my pain,

without
understanding the scars

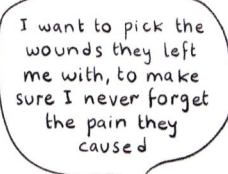

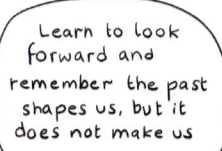

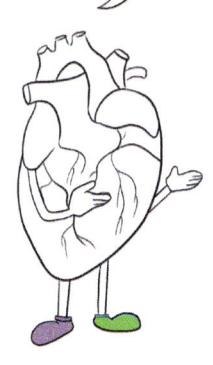

The silence of grief

Grief muddles my mind; I feel stupid and slow
The pain and frustration are bigger than I've ever known

I forget the things I didn't even know were possible
Memories coming and going seem unstoppable

The good and the bad seem to slip away
How did I end up this way?

One moment, I want to be truly alone
And in the next, I want your guiding hand in the unknown

My mind cannot be made
and when darkness beckons,

can I be saved?

The ever-changing tide

This elusive word is
a painful art

Subjective, hard to describe,
tearing our world apart

A minute, a day,
or a year

The memory of you
still fills me with pain and tears

When do these
waves subside?

My emotions coming and
going like a changing tide

Like the sea, it can be a beautiful,
yet dangerous thing

Contrasting emotions is
something grief brings

Though the pain may
fade in our hearts

The memories we cherish,
mean we will never be far apart

Love and grief

Life's ebbs and flows
The darkness making me a stranger I no longer know

Loss has shown me the depth of love
And answers for loss are often something I cannot think of

They live in my thoughts but are no longer here
Their absence casting a shadow that fills me with fear

My world is left in pieces
But people have promised that the pain decreases

And that we can learn to live with our hardest loss
Embracing the hurt, is something I am trying to get across

When love appears, so can grief
It leaves question marks around our beliefs

Our belief as to whether it's a fair exchange
When we lose this person, our world will permanently change

The echo of lost presence

Do we truly understand
the definition of loss

Death doesn't define this
message I am trying to get across

Loss includes those who
are no longer part of your storyline

Your mind whispers, it's not a matter
of when, but a matter of time

They used to be someone
to go to for guidance

Now, when you call,
the phone rings and ends in a deafening silence

A silence so loud that it
reminds you of what was

It leaves the question
they left my life because?

The cracks in our foundations

A loss that extended
to my best friend

When I processed our time together,
I thought this pain would end

The loss was
on so many levels

We had love,
but not the fundamentals

We have our own
paths to own

I know my feelings
were sporadic and unknown

We tried what we
thought was a new start

But sometimes past memories
can be too painful for the heart

It's clear to see we
have both grown

Sometimes it's important to
reflect and cherish time alone

From my heart, I wish you all
the best in your journey

When it comes to processing loss,
you can never be late or early

The unspoken cost

Do we ever
talk about family

we once called
our own

where the love
that was created,
now sits

alone...

My family tree

As each branch fell,
I started to break too

The days passed,
and so did you

How could I recognise life,
when pain obstructs the view?

Reflection

You closed
the chapter
and wrote the
last line

But I forgave
the author
and showed
the world

I am doing just fine...

When empathy fails

You will get better, be strong

When I describe myself with this word,
it feels so wrong

They are in a better place

My mind is dark and it feels like it
can never be in a happy space

It's been a while, get over it

Time doesn't mean I'm healing and
that's something I'm scared to admit

You're young, so you won't understand

Ok tell me how I live without
their guiding hand?

I know exactly how you feel

Then give me answers on how you
think I'm going to heal

Life goes on

I'm sorry, peace and happiness isn't
something I will suddenly stumble upon...

Grieving the unattainable

Sometimes, people won't become
the person you needed

Your expectations of them
were never something that was exceeded

When did perfection
become so attainable

Having this view on future
partners is not sustainable

When you grieved,
what was it for?

Was it your constant
want for more?

When pain becomes peace

It used to be a storm that raged within,
now it's a quiet acceptance that
allowed the work to begin

I came to shift my perspectives,
being thankful for what I had
was far more effective

Thinking about everything that could've been,
was one way to stop my
present day being seen

I learnt to worry less about what I could not change,
pain for peace seemed
like a fair exchange

Acceptance is about finding a way,
to live with the love and
memories every day

So, I'll move forward with new views and an open heart,
honouring the past,
but allowing a fresh start

The gift between pain and loss

It's sad our paths
may never cross

But going separate ways
didn't just give us loss

It was so much more
profound than that

You opened my world,
a statement, and a fact

You gave me the
gift of travel

Showing me this breathtaking
world that I am yet to unravel

So, I say, it's never as
simple as loss or pain

You transformed the path of my life,
and it will never be the same again

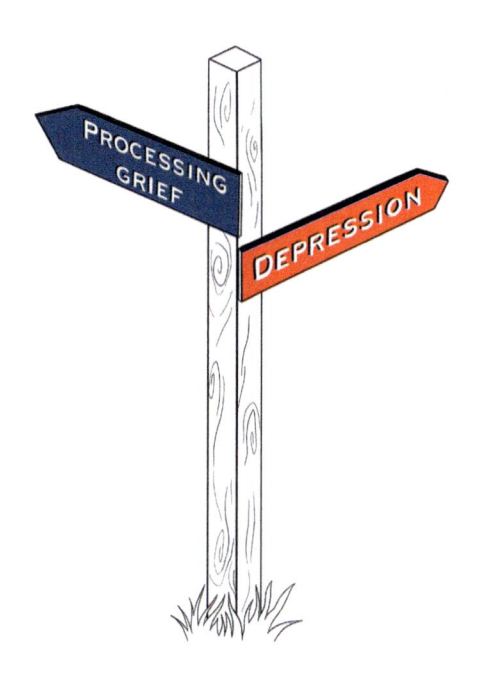

Depression

Depression was a mystery to me. A dark feeling that followed me everywhere, dimming even the brightest of moments. It left me asking whether this was just sadness or something more significant. Despite the unwavering smile and the appearance of being the life of the party, it sharply contrasted with the internal battle raging within my mind. A constant stream of emotions that I seemingly could not understand. The more I tried to make sense of it all, the more it felt like a never-ending spiral. When did this begin, and when would it end?

The internal battle was exhausting, and it was always easier for me to shut down. To protect myself from the hurt and loss I had created in my head. Situations I had explored a million times over gave me more unanswered questions and more in-explainable behaviours. Being closed off gave me a mask to hide behind. The smile being a temporary distraction from the prevailing emptiness. It diverted my attention, allowing me to live two lives simultaneously. These lives presented themselves at opposite ends of my emotional spectrum.

I can vividly remember a conversation before the 24th of October 2021 with a trusted friend. We sat in the car, and it felt like a more manageable environment to talk in. The lack of eye contact made it somewhat less intense. It softened the words that were being spoken in a way. The person across from me had noticed patterns in my behaviours and emotions, an absence in my being. The sadness in my eyes could be seen outside, the constant tiredness and lack of sleep. My mind didn't want to believe what they said was true, but deep down, I knew it was. My new reality.

Even with this realisation, I chose to ignore the words of advice. For me, familiarity could be found in the depths of depression. Almost a bias toward finding comfort in the darkness. It felt as though it had become a companion. My mind felt trapped in a never-ending cycle, unable to break free from the grip it had on me.

Coming to terms with my depression was a process of acceptance. Acceptance that it had taken hold of me physically and mentally and

I had lost myself. But with time and professional support, I realised that darkness was, in fact, part of me, as was my trauma and pain. It was an acceptance that I did not need to rid myself of these thoughts, but instead, I needed to understand them better. To revisit memories and moments and come to peace with them. It was a journey of many dips and hurdles but one supported by the love of those around me.

This unwavering need to overcome something I had lived with for so long made me look back and reflect on my journey. Unpicking behaviours from my past and understanding that what I had learnt wasn't necessarily the definition of right or wrong. And how these definitions were ultimately mine to explore and understand. The morality of my thoughts and emotions was questioned as I tried to connect the two sides of me. The disconnect between my external appearance and inner turmoil was all too real.

The poems in this chapter resonate with a strength that cannot be ignored. I once believed that depression was permanent and could never be overcome. It took extensive self-reflection and compassion to find answers and lead me to the inner peace that existed beyond my dark days.

Tracing the veins of darkness

My time with
depression

A deep dive into this
word is now in session

Unique in the way it steals
the words you want to say

Slowly drawing on your energy,
day by day

I was closed in my life
and my views

A deep, dark space,
where I was lost and confused

It took a commitment
that never faded

To understand the darkness
and pain in stages

It created a new start
and a new end

Where light was discovered in
a place where darkness was my closest friend...

Unfinished sentences

In each fleeting moment, I could not pinpoint what I was
I could never finish the sentence; I felt this way because?

depression became my entire world
Each day was defined by this abrupt word

I was pretending to be someone new as each day passed
This wasn't a fleeting feeling; it was here to last

lost and alone were emotions that became very real
An absence of feeling showed my past was yet to heal

It was just me, **myself,** and I
In loneliness, how do I wave this version of me goodbye?

Beyond the label

Does a label give you answers
or a box to work within?

Or does a label give you
answers to let the work begin?

Does a label allow you to
work through this in your own individual way?

Or does the label give you a
checklist of when you're supposed to be ok?

Does a label give you
definitions that lets you speak with others?

Or does the label give you answers
that leave your mind smothered?

You see, depression is a word
that is discussed a lot

But remember, a circle doesn't
have to fit in a square slot...

Accepting the past and re-writing the future

Today, a new chapter, a new start

Today, a true connection between your mind and heart

Today, a day where you held your head high

Today, a day where your smile wasn't a lie

Today, a day where you celebrated your true self

Today, a day where you prioritised your mental health

Today, a new day and a chance to change your tomorrow...

My inner self-destruction

The outlook was
sad and alone

I hated everything that
remained in the unknown

How did those around me
see this version of me

No one realised I could hide
my struggles to this degree

I labelled it,
an illness, and a curse

A feeling that left my smile
feeling a little rehearsed

Bright eyes and
a beaming smile

Both of these things showed glimpses of hope,
everyone once in a while

That was the battle
each and every day

Depression told me enduring
this pain was 'okay'

It had taken over
my being

A world of pain,
that only I was seeing

My false promises

It had taken
its toll

With the final cost
being my fragmented soul

I learnt that tomorrow
can often be too late

Depression was a crushing
and uncontrollable weight

It called time and my
tomorrow wasn't to be seen

I would become a
discarded memory,

*A what
could've been...*

When memories turn to tears

If a memory still inflicts pain within
The pain will become physical, as tears roll down your skin

Your vision blurs and sadness takes over your mind
The reason for this feeling remains undefined

When we don't have answers or understanding
Our mind is troubled, but our body is still standing

That's the key with anything mental
The fact we can hide our pain so well isn't coincidental

It's a struggle to find the words for what we feel
Being open with them makes them feel more real

Being real means accepting this is where we are
How did our mental state slip this far?

The crushing weight of my insignificance

What truly defines the
life I am living

Intrusive thoughts are
something my mind is giving

I can't sleep as I don't
want a temporary silence

Am I looking for something
bigger than guidance

Love surrounds me
but I fail to see it

It's something my
mind no longer permits

My self-worth has
hit rock bottom

And I just want to be
ignored and forgotten

Is it such a
small ask

To become a
presence in your past...

Light will help reunite

The darkness
A weary mind is unable to see the light shining through

The darkness
A weary mind has left every part of my past under review

The darkness
Intrusive thoughts engulf my days

The darkness
Intrusive thoughts distract my mind in harmful ways

The darkness
Pain is felt in every social situation

The darkness
Pain is something left to interpretation

You see, the darkness can
be broken with a light

When we love ourselves,
the change is a beautiful sight

Harnessing the strength of inner silence

Sometimes we
need to be alone

It helps explore the thoughts
that are buried deep in the unknown

The cloud often appears
when we enter this space

Our thoughts begin to
spiral at an uncontrollable pace

Depression and anxiety
are a painful mix

It leaves you trying to explore
scenarios that you can never fix

A negative spin is taken on
each painful reflection

Seeing the same memory again
and again, fails to give you direction

The darkness then
comes over me

I close my eyes,
imagining the light that I may one day see

It's what helped them...

Be grateful for what exists today
But in my mind, I can't see the happiness on display

I'm not going to walk on eggshells around you
I'm sorry, I promise I am trying to see this through

You were doing so well before
I know, I struggle to want to live anymore

Things could be so much worse
I want to move forward but I feel like I am stuck in reverse

You are surrounded by support and love
Trust me, not being able to feel this is something I am aware of

It's what will help you

In my mind, I can't see the happiness on display
Live presently and celebrate progress day by day

I'm sorry, I promise I am trying to see this through
This is a journey of starting something new

I know, I struggle to want to live anymore
Voice your feelings; they are not something you should ignore

I want to move forward, but I feel like I am stuck in reverse
Pressuring yourself on direction will only make this worse

How about if I want to cut this life short
It's a sign you need professional support

A new chapter is waiting for this version of you
The journey is never straight, but you will see this through

A fragile balance

I still think my emotions
are confused

Because when joy arrives,
a troubled mind ensues

I ask whether this is just a
distraction from the pain

And whether these bursts of
happiness will ever feel the same

Here alone with
my thoughts

Trying to recall everything
I've been taught

*Be kind to your
mind* they say

Address your inner child
and say it's going to be ok

Give yourself a
moment to breathe

As this moment will pass,
and you'll turn over a new leaf

Discovering brightness in fading colours

Sadness is an
emotion we feel

Whereas depression is a lack of feeling,
showing us the pain that is yet to heal

It is complicated
by name

And the final symptom is
ending the mental pain

Ask yourself,
how great can life be?

A world awaits,
there is so much to experience and see

I want you to think about
the love that surrounds you

There is a way
you can see this through

The world is a better
place with you here

And all I ask is that you give
yourself a chance to persevere

Does time heal wounds?

Learn to let
go

And let the river
of life flow

This is about
loving yourself

As peace in the mind
is the highest form of wealth

Address your
emotional history

To avoid the reason behind
your spiralling being a mystery

Follow your
intuition

And give yourself permission
to start this healthy mission

Falling in love with each of life's seasons

It can be likened to the weather
It starts with now and ends in forever

An immeasurable thing
That will never pre-warn you with what it brings

Like a snowflake, no two are the same
The only similarity is in the name

Remember, recovery has not got a time scale
It's not a test that can be passed or failed

In the same way, weather comes and goes
You will experience some highs and some lows

Waves create a ripple effect

When we let the river of life flow
We can see how freedom can give us a certain glow

Life is full of twists and turns with no timeframes
They say it's only a lesson if wisdom is what we gain

You see, pain can often hold us prisoner in our past
Letting go and becoming peaceful is no easy task

It's amazing how negative thoughts can erode a smile
So let your mind be present and free every once in a while

Seed to strength

A seed that was ready to flower
The circle of life, where water and light hold the power

These two elements were an enemy, not a friend
As darkness became my most familiar dead-end

The seed represented what light life could bring
But below the surface, love within was not a familiar thing

I searched for the water and the light
But happiness was unreachable and out of sight

The stem reached above the surface, tired and alone
Too weak to support an exploration of the unknown

But roots started to appear when I started to ask
I'm broken and need help dealing with my broken past

A dormant seed then became a beautiful flower
Where vulnerability was my saviour, an unspoken superpower

Redefining 'I'm fine'

When I glance back in time
I realised how much I used to say the words, I'm fine

It's a unique answer in a way
Confirming good or bad was simply something I couldn't say

It was a practiced evasion, a skilled retreat
A strategy that worked whilst being so discreet

But as I reflect, and this chapter comes to a close
I have found peace with the unknown

So, here's to a clearer day and a brighter tomorrow
We end with positivity but started with sorrow

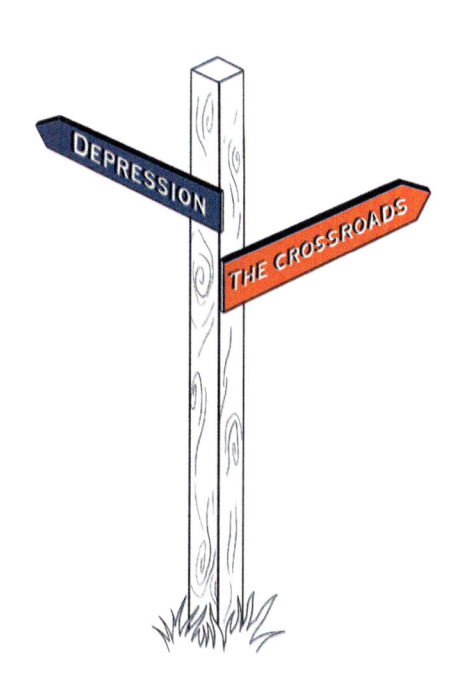

The crossroads

October 24th, 2021, 16:49. A moment burned in my memory forever. The moment when my world came to a close. The moment I wanted to put an end to the pain that had been suffocating me for so long. The moment when every path ahead felt like a dead end.

For some time, my mind had been calling time on my existence. And on that day, at that moment, I had a plan. A plan to escape what I felt was an inescapable pain. I had been sitting in my car for some time, alone. My phone rang. I let the call run and it went to the answerphone. A voicemail appeared:

I know you probably don't want to talk to me, but, um, I really need to talk to you, um, so please, if you can, please give me a buzz back, even if it is briefly...

This was the turning point. There was a shakiness in the voice of the person calling. They had been close to my struggles. They had tried to show me love when it wasn't something I felt I could recognise at that time. The moment I chose to call back was the moment I chose a different path. A path of facing up to what had placed me in this situation. An honesty to those who cared that I was at breaking point. For the first time, I embraced them as the true me.

Tears streamed down my face. This was the first time someone had seen me break down in my adult years. The first time I had openly shown my self-harm scars. It was the moment I had been so scared of, and instead of people thinking of me as weak, they pulled me in tighter as I presented the true Ben.

Suicide can be seen as such a sensitive word. More often than not, whispered and avoided. Almost as if speaking it aloud brings the darkness closer. For me, it was a decision resulting from the intense mental pain I was feeling – a pain hidden behind, and one that the naked eye could not see. And yet, it was a pain that was so incredibly real.

Why does society often struggle to talk about suicide? Why does it leave behind a legacy of questions and often guilt? Why does it feel like a taboo subject? I have struggled with these questions for so long and hope that speaking out will bring some normality that this is something we can work through and that it is ok to reach out and ask for help.

The safety that I sought for my mind and soul should have been found in the arms of my loved ones. But instead, it was found in the idea of death and ending my pain. The thoughts of suicide became my safe haven. People say that if someone knew how much they were loved, they wouldn't choose to end their life. But what if that person struggles to feel the love? What if they have never let themselves truly experience what love is? These questions have lingered in my mind, and I believe it's important that this topic is explored and understood.

As I sit here and revisit my journey with suicidal thoughts, the memories flood my mind with intense emotions. It was a dark and painful time when I believed the world would be better off without me. The emptiness and loneliness were suffocating. I vividly recall the moment when the mental struggles became physical, and I explored this experience in a poem titled 'Self-Harm Makes Mental Health Physical.'

Looking back, I realise the effort it took to show and portray happiness when I felt the opposite emotions inside. How could I show two opposing emotions at the same time? How could I be so consumed with death yet still put on a happy face for those around me? The reality of suicidal thoughts is that they are blunt, both in their intensity and the way they impact every aspect of life. Friendships, relationships, and even family are all affected. And as I look back on my journey, I ask myself, how did I get here? How did I reach a point where death seemed like the only answer?

A deep and all-encompassing darkness plagued my experience with depression. It clouded every aspect of my life like a pair of sunglasses that never came off. The world was vibrant and full of life, but my mind couldn't grasp it, so I protected myself with a filter that distorted the happiness around me.

The journey to seeking help to understand my suicidal thoughts was one of the toughest challenges I've ever faced. Despite knowing I needed help, the thought of taking that first step was overwhelming. I was consumed by anxiety and fear of the unknown, questioning whether talking to someone would actually make a difference.

I eventually mustered the courage to book my first therapy session, but the nerves remained. As the call started, my heart was racing. The therapist asked a simple question about how I felt about not seeing my family during the COVID-19 pandemic, and suddenly, the floodgates opened. Tears streamed down my face as I struggled to express my emotions. It was a stark realisation of how closed off I had become, continually fearing judgment and anxiety about revealing my vulnerability.

I often found myself concentrating on concealing my tears rather than confronting the root of what was causing them. It took a life-altering moment, a brush with death, to finally let my guard down and show my true self in therapy. Although therapy is a beautiful, constructive thing, I had to practise what I was learning. In the same way, we train our muscles, I had to learn to train my mind in new and more empathetic ways.

Present

It felt as though my
personality was split in two,
Once a young boy who thought
he could see this through

you constantly search for the
answer in your mind,
learning that as time goes on,
your fate is now sealed and signed

to feel **love**d but so alone was
a confusing thing,
people said 'you need to help
yourself and let your journey to recovery begin'

It was hard to understand how
that journey could start,
the thought of exploring my
past felt like it would tear me apart

resting and reflecting wasn't
something I could master,
I constantly questioned
will this road end in disaster'?

I knew it was only a matter
of time before I **fall**,
my mental health wasn't
getting better, and I'd hit a wall

Getting **into** the rhythm of hiding
my true self was part of the plan,
I was in a **place** no one
could understand

Be a man

The world dictates
what we should be

It's like having this
title means strength is guaranteed

People say you are the
happiest in the room

It's scary how people see a
consistent smile and assume

A tormented mind can
be hidden so well

People don't see the true you,
until you end the living hell

The final symptom explains
how fake that smile was

They ask the question;
he ended his life because?

It's a sentence no
one can truly get right

The struggle was so personal,
and it was me and my mind in the final fight

Maybe the definition of
being a man should change

Showing emotion and speaking
out doesn't have to feel strange

M _ N U P

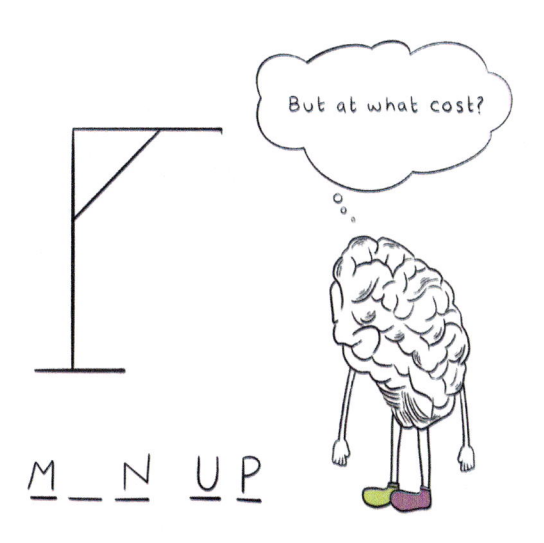

But at what cost?

The crossroads

When we talk about the word
commit it sounds like a crime

When actually, it's our
mental struggles calling time

We can't live the life we
have today any longer

As our minds are at their lowest low,
and can't get any stronger

The indescribable pain
can't be put into words

And it makes the line
between life and death a little blurred

Do we exist when we
find safety in the darkness

Our minds tangled,
a confusing mess

Please trust that there is
a new life waiting for you

It's important you explore
your pain and see this through

Seek help, for it will be the
biggest and most significant stride

Reflect, take a deep breath,
and let love and hope become your guide

Ending life or ending a life

My mind was so closed to
an option that wasn't death

Ending life or ending a life was
never considered in the same breath

I did not understand that there
was a new life to start

My heart and the word
happiness felt worlds apart

I never saw that this decision
didn't have to be final

My life replicated a broken
needle on a vinyl

The soundtrack gradually
becoming less clear

A shadow arrived,
and it filled me with fear....

Cultivating kindness in the midst of despair

My mind insists,
I've had enough, no more

Yet the pain deepens,
shaking me to my core

The game of life
is mine to play

Depression will whisper,
do you want to stay?

It felt like I was trying
to be so strong

But everything in this harsh
world seemed to go wrong

I had to learn to be kind
to my fragile heart

As this is where life's journey begins,
a safe place to start…

Self-harm makes mental health physical

Self-harm can be
physical or mental,
the similarities with the
word harm isn't coincidental

One is pain,
hidden under the skin,
the other is when the mental
struggles can't be held within

It's a distraction from
the mind's visit to the past,
brighter days are coming,
and these intrusive thoughts are not here to last

Be kind to yourself when
you process those memories,
as I know when the blade beckons,
it whispers, *do you remember me?*

Each step can begin with
love from within,
be kind to yourself and let
your journey to a happier self-begin

A call for help

Our heads try to listen
But the voice tells us this is the path of most men

We forget that it's ok to speak out
The final symptom is often our last shout

Would the world accept these tears
Or does the phone call become the last thing you hear?

How can we change this heart-breaking storyline
It begins with us not telling everyone *we're fine*

People want you here in the today
And they want to hear the words you have to say

The outcome relies on what you choose to do
With the right support, you can see this through

You will find answers in the past
And once these are discovered, the pain won't be here to last

The light at the end of the tunnel is yours to ignite
Your days will be lighter, and your discoveries bright

On the other side

I was proud I could use my
own experiences to help you

The struggles I'd faced helped
 you see this through

In the darkest hour, I was able
to show you the love that you couldn't see

I'd never seen mental pain
outside of myself to this degree

Hours felt like minutes
in those moments

Self-love was the
missing component

It's never about blame or
feeling misunderstood

But letting them explore,
to embrace themselves as they should

Snakes and ladders

A ladder appears and you grip tight
You just want an out, no matter if it's wrong or right

You wanted to leave life to a roll of the dice
A final finish, an ending so precise

The snakes whisper to you along the way
"Don't leave the old you behind, we want him to stay"

I mutter that I am trying to rise, not fall
To love myself and try and stand tall

But they ask, *"isn't pain all you know?"*
"let that fake smile become your final show"

The curtain that doesn't close

With mental health, there's two
outcomes that show their face

One erases your tomorrow,
a final embrace

The darkness comes
over you like a tide

A painful narrative,
a painful internal guide

I know love and light
is uncomfortable terrain

But it can build new bridges,
new roads, to ease the strain

Put trust in this
uncertain quest

As your curtain is not ready to close,
to be laid to rest

Pain hurts,
but love always wins

It's down to you,
and how this journey begins

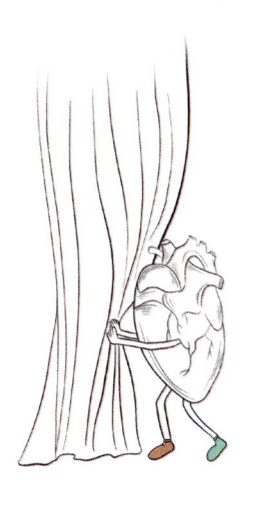

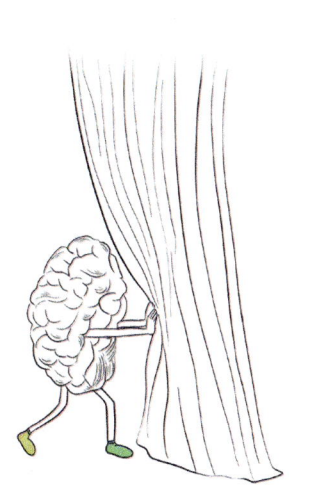

When we choose life

We talked through the
labyrinth that was your heart

Where love was pain,
and pain was art

The darkness was your
safest retreat

A piece of you was taken,
leaving you incomplete

And like this poem,
there isn't an answer or a true end

The darkness was a toxic lover,
and now the light is your friend

After and before

Suicide is a
permanent solution

That as an illness ends
our chance for evolution

It's heartbreaking
when you hear the news

As a period of hurt
and confusion ensues

We wonder and try and
understand what happened in their mind

The little voice,
cruel and unkind

If you're trapped in
this thought today

Seek help,
as I promise it's going to be ok

I know asking for help
is a massive step for you

There may not be a way past,
but I promise there's a way through

Don't worry about
the thoughts of others

This story is about you
and how you recover

Ladders and snakes

My heartbeat had almost hit zero
But someone called, my own ladder, my own hero

As the snakes continued to whisper to me
I realised this wasn't the man I wanted to be

I faced the voices in my mind
Changing my own narrative with something kind

Life can sometimes be down to a roll of the dice
Where with pain, we have to live through it twice

But to replace pain with peace
Is a life-altering release

So, although the game of life has twists and turns
you're still here to experience the many lessons you will learn

The triangle

I cried for the first time
in front of you

Your supporting gaze told
me you'd help me see this through

Depression had
taken all of the light

Yet you stood firm,
guiding me through my darkest night

The love you gave,
etched in my memory

Paving the way for me
to become the man I always wanted to be

The circle

In the beginning, there
were four

They had never seen this
version of me before

There were glimpses of the
hurt I was feeling

My eyes showed the joy
that depression was stealing

I hid my struggles
incredibly well

But on this day,
I waved my old life farewell

I trusted my support circle
with my life in those moments

I realised that being open
about my struggles was the missing component

The circle showed me that
this version of me could be loved

I poured my heart out
without being judged

The journey was
mine to explore

But this wouldn't have started
without my magical four

Lost in my own maze

The crossroads transformed
a once broken trail

A new path was formed with
a love that wasn't destined to fail

Resilience was created
from my battles within

A new life was ready to start,
the next chapter ready to begin

The 24th of October now stands
as a powerful sign

And a reminder of my journey,
each chapter now redefined

So, although these pages are filled
with hurt and pain

New perspectives have helped
ensure I never see that side of my world again

Helping Yesterday's Self

Hindsight can be both a blessing and a curse. As I explored the past and present, I questioned my paths and choices. This chapter, however, is not about regret but more about challenging behaviours that once held me captive. Moments of hope, snippets of advice, and meaningful words to inspire my future self.

When I reflect on my past, I can't help but be amazed by its impact on my present. The songs I listened to in the darker days of my life, and the poems I wrote, all served as a haven for me in their own unique way. The way our past clings to us is both mysterious and fascinating. Whether that's a person, music, scents, or experiences, the past shaped me. However, the extent of its influence on my present is a choice I make every day.

As I delved into the labyrinth of my mind, I used to find my past holding a curious power over me. The familiarity of what had happened was known to me, comforting almost. But as I grew, I realised that my memory could have been more reliable. My mind was unconsciously shielding itself from the truth, almost as if it was afraid of facing it. A fear that the pain of it all was too much to bear.

The torment in my mind, in many instances, was imaginary. Anxious thoughts created heartache and suffering that never actually occurred. I would conjure up scenarios and live through them as if they were real. Irrational thoughts of betrayal or losing someone I loved caused me to push them away. I was consumed by the intensity of these emotions. I foolishly began to place my happiness on several external factors, such as having a certain amount of money, a particular job, or a specific lifestyle.

When it came to buying or achieving things, I was always left feeling unfulfilled or disconnected. That was when the realisation about baseline happiness struck me - the understanding that, after a significant event, we often return to our original state of contentment. This was when I learnt that adopting positive habits and making some lifestyle changes was going to be a big part of my recovery and long-term happiness.

Another key cornerstone in my recovery was acknowledging my lack of self-compassion and forgiveness. Instead of trying to understand my struggles or mistakes, I focused more on berating myself for having made them. Within that mindset existed a deep self-criticism and hatred. After a lot of self-reflection and working with my therapist, I can now look back at my past self with the kindness and respect that I deserved.

I've come to understand that every behaviour had a protective function crucial to my survival at the time. The criticism has been replaced by gratitude for the resilience of my past self. Now, I hold space for both, accepting and loving that version of myself whilst actively working towards personal growth and evolution.

Self-forgiveness is an ongoing mission which releases me from the guilt, shame and other negative emotions which burdened me for much of my early adult life. I've learnt to embrace my imperfections as a natural part of the human experience and extend the same compassion to myself that I readily offer to others. My mistakes do not define my inherent value and the freedom this has brought me has been transformative.

A journey, not a battle

If you never
stop fighting

do you
ever win?

or do you
need to accept

that peace
in pain,

is where life truly begins?

Whispered opportunities

A voice spoken,
is a voice heard

A story told,
is a story remembered

A door opened,
is a door entered

Speaking out
is not self-centred

A message sent,
is a message received

As men, we can learn to grieve

Alone but empowered

A house doesn't
make a home

This is a space where
I've felt loved and alone

I went back and
re-processed my past

In my darkest hours, I wasn't
sure how long the pain would last

Sometimes it's hard
to see through the clouds

Let me remind you that
sitting in them is allowed

Give yourself the time to
feel what you are

As when you look back,
you'll wonder how you've come this far

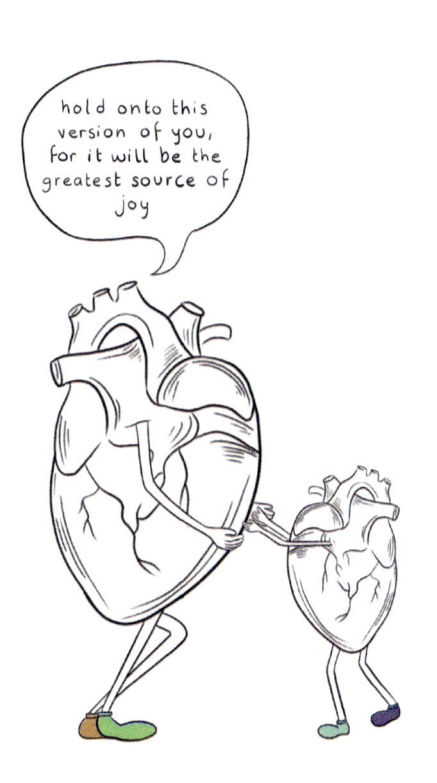

Rethinking inner fulfilment

We go through life
setting massive goals

But forget to ask what
is good for our souls?

If our expectations
go unmet

We see this as a
cause for upset

Do we sit back and ask
whether we are being realistic?

Or do we let ourselves
become another statistic

So many of our
New Year's goals fail

Which is failure on a
massive scale

Should we be kinder to
ourselves with our expectations

And spend more time
reviewing our aspirations

Light in her tears

Value is not just how
your body appears

Your gaze meets your reflection,
and you are consumed by tears

It's about embracing who
you are in this moment

Live presently,
adore your reflection and own it

Who has the right to tell
you what perfection entails

Acceptance of self is the true
beauty that will always prevail

Society decides on the words
we associate with our appearance

Do we need to learn how to love
ourselves without interference?

Immeasurable

Wealth,
what an elusive word

Wealth,
is it owned or simply transferred?

Wealth,
pursued in a relentless race

Wealth,
an immeasurable space

Wealth,
does it justify our worth?

Wealth,
does it place us in a hierarchy on this earth?

Wealth,
what if it could be found within?

Wealth,
when we place value on ourselves, that's when balance begins

In gaining everything, I forgot I am now left with nothing

Depression

You hate me,
berate me,
and slate me,

but you will
never break me...

Drive or destroy

You see, it takes drive to recover
from disappointment in your today

Reassure yourself and say
it's not a bad life, it's a bad day

Disappointment can often
be linked to the expectations we set

Being kind to yourself is
something we often forget

Take a moment to reflect on
what's in front of you

Your future is waiting and
wants you to see this through

Time

A hard concept
to grasp

As we often get
hung up on our past

But when we choose
to live in the today

It's easier to
find our way

You see, the present is
called the present for a reason

We can find joy in the
simple changes in seasons

Social media's lens can
show us that we're behind in life

But comparing constantly
isn't right

You are you today
and that's simply enough

You don't need to compare
against all of this other stuff

Each moment will
never be the same

And when you can appreciate the now,
life is yours to reclaim

The weight of unresolved pain

The longer we carry something,
the heavier it starts to get

It sinks into our unconscious,
a memory we cannot forget

It can whisper in the shadows
of the mind

A harmful thought,
something painful and unkind

Rediscovery around what matters

When do we end this material chase
We consume and want at an unbelievable pace

Is success justified by the size of the box you live within
As if more rooms are where true joy begins

What if we focused on the thing we can never get back
Money is never going to fix the things you lack

Time is the true currency of our lives
So why do we spend most of our days creating financial ties

Ties to living outside our means
We are scared of robots but can be likened to machines

Machines that follow the path life should take
Remember, it's called a lesson, not one big mistake

Behaviours and the heart

Understanding your
behaviours is just the start

It's about that mind-body
connection with the heart

As we delve into the
unconscious mind

Our being becomes
more aligned

Less unexplained
behaviours appear

Your thoughts become less clouded,
and your vision more clear

In darkness, we cannot
see the beauty in front of us

The light shines through
when we begin to trust

A trust that believes life
is not one linear journey

Let me tell you, in this world,
you are neither late nor early

The line between love and loss

Today, a memory appeared
A moment with someone I used to hold dear

We sat in the warmth of the fire
Our hearts filled with love, our eyes with desire

Your gaze met mine
A connection filled with magic, something so divine

So, although our paths may never cross
There is a message I want to get across

There are memories that lie between love and loss

The coffee shop

A little retreat,
a window to the world,
a front-row seat

Moments of silence, moments of laughter
people coming and going,
chapter after chapter

So, as I observe this frantic race
I realise,
I have found my happy place

Peaceful and content
a pause with a coffee,
time well spent

In my silence

You fought battles
no one could see

You embraced the
man you used to be

You grew and showed
patience within

You overcame and struggled,
allowing peace to begin

You loved and
you healed

Not making masculinity
your perfect shield

You loved and
you gave

When you realised it was you,
you had to save

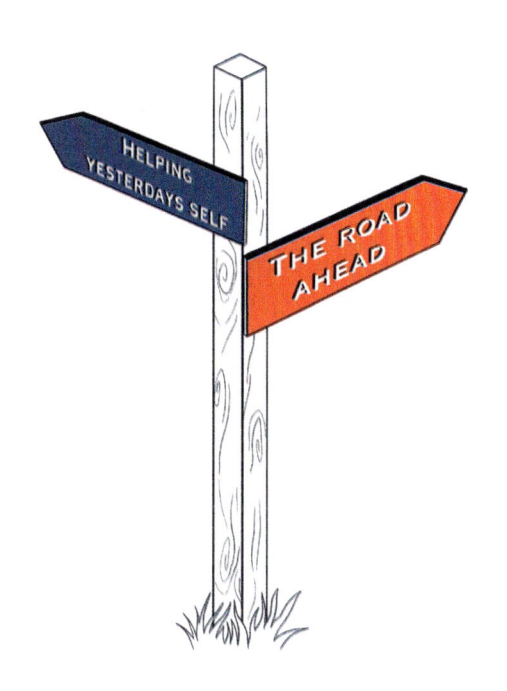

The Road Ahead

I can't help but appreciate the power of one step. One step led me to answer the phone when I had chosen to end my life. One step allowed the most broken version of me to be seen. And in being seen, I was able to begin my healing journey. It has been a journey of deep and intense questioning, asking - how did I end up here? Why was this the answer?

Amidst this exploration, a crucial decision emerged: the choice not to run from my pain anymore. It was part of me, and in running from it, I was running from the most authentic version of myself. The transformative shift occurred when I embraced my mistakes, reframing them as valuable lessons. Rather than allowing my past to tear me down, I committed to learning from it and carrying those profound lessons into what I now affectionately term my 'bonus years'.

In searching for this new life I wanted to live, I first had to understand and relearn certain behaviours. I quickly realised the 'understanding' I was seeking was expansive and continuously evolving. My desire to understand was never about a need to reach the end of my self-discovery journey. I recognise that this is an ongoing journey marked by adaptation, change and continuous learning.

Within this process of adaptation, I found myself questioning my perception of masculinity. I had the stark realisation that part of my journey to this dark place had been fuelled by my need to embody strength and endure battles alone because that's what society expects of men. The consequences of this mindset were almost death, prompting me to promise to myself that the person I was that day would cease to exist. From then on, my inner mantra became, you can end a life without ending a life.

I can clearly remember that a few days after I tried to end my life, I mustered the strength to return to the gym. I felt so deeply weak and confused about how something mental could so deeply impact my body. But it was me presenting true to who I was at that moment, broken. A dear friend asked if I was ok, to which I replied yes, but he persisted and asked again. It may not have changed the world, but that moment changed mine. The second time, I answered honestly, and we proceeded to have a deeply honest conversation about where I was. It opened a beautiful connection. So, to all of the people who ask twice, you are changing the world for that one person, I promise.

In connecting with others, it inspired connection within, and art became my medium of exploration. Poetry for me was less about right or wrong, and instead about a journey—a way to connect thoughts in gentle but thought-provoking ways. A way to express the inexpressible. A way to ride the waves rather than being drowned by them. It also gave me waypoints and markers on this healing journey.

The contrast that exists in the man who started this book is stark. It is funny; I often refer to myself as a child again in many respects, as the 24th October marks my 'rebirth', making me almost three years old once more. In this, a profound sense of playfulness thrives, allowing me to find joy in the simplest of things and transforming ordinary moments into extraordinary experiences, overflowing with happiness and wonder.

Often, I find myself sitting atop the tree stump, reflecting on the innocence of the boy who once sat there in the moment from my childhood. It was much the same at the crossroads, in a way. A moment suspended in time, surrounded by a silence that only I could break.

Both times, a subconscious part of my mind recognised, or at least hoped, that someone would sense my vulnerability and disorientation, fearing that if I was left alone for too long, I might not survive. Perhaps the significance of the voicemail which catalysed this whole narrative, was that instead of navigating through the vast forest of my thoughts alone, someone reached out, forged a connection and offered me a chance to embrace a new perspective and find support in the community that existed around me.

THE ROAD AHEAD

MEET THE AUTHOR

Meet the Author

Where do I start? A unicorn in human form? I have the uniqueness without the magic. Ginger with blue eyes, apparently one of the rarest combinations in a human. It feels as though I have won the genetic lottery but with more sun cream.

Writing is very much something I stumbled upon, a path untravelled that has now become one of my fondest places to explore. My writing, coupled with my golden retriever-like energy, makes for a unique mix of prose and poetry. It really all began during the early days of my recovery when I made a pact with vulnerability.

Within this was a simple rule: I would not retire to my bedroom until my mind found peace or at least less shaky ground to stand on. I have referenced one of my earliest memories of getting lost in a forest in my introduction and this moment has stuck with me. Many nights were spent walking around my local area, listening to random YouTube videos that spoke about the basics behind some of our most powerful emotions.

It makes me smile when I think of how passers-by would view me as I smiled, laughed, and cried. However, these walks were a safe space where I could be candid with myself. Moments where I allowed my thoughts to flow freely, finding joy in the simplest of details. The rain, the sun, the rustling of leaves, and the endless parade of adorable doggos that trotted past me.

When it came to note-taking, I did not care for time or place. Whether I had woken up in the middle of the night or between sets at the gym, I would jot down ideas and revelations I had thought of. And let me tell you, I am as surprised as you are that these thoughts have turned into a whole damn book!

You may be wondering who I am outside of this journey. I am a lover of everything sport and feel as though I am the living embodiment of all the gear and no idea. My intense focus on trying new sports has left me considerably average at many different things. And of course, whether it is snowboarding or mountain biking, I like to look the part to make up for the sheer absence of any remote talent!

So, here's to my last chapter and my final verse. After all, this journey starts with the mind and ends with something kind...

A heartfelt thank you

There are too many to name, but I am forever grateful to those who have loved and supported me through this journey. All of the calls, catch-ups, and walks have never been forgotten and will forever be moments for which I am deeply thankful for. My siblings, my incredible friends, and furry friends, of course, I love you from the absolute bottom of my heart.

To my sister, my best friend, and my editor. All of the words I wanted to say, I have. Thank you for picking me up in times of doubt and struggle. Your calmness and honesty within this journey have been beyond special. I simply could not have done this without you.

To the magical four. In my deepest, darkest hours, you accepted the most broken version of me. I love you all and will never forget the words of encouragement and care you showed me. Entwined in the words of this book are your words of advice, your love, and your care. You embraced the most broken version of me and, in turn, inspired me to do the same. Our paths may have changed, but the memories never will.

My platonic soulmate, where do I start, and where do I begin? Your unwavering support and love is threaded into all the words that exist in these pages. Through the tears and through the sadness, you have always been there. Your directness and deep-rooted honesty lifted me from some of the darkest days of my life. Thank you for being my light.

To my dear friend Doc, I may not have known you for a lifetime, but you have given me a lifetime of lessons. The kindness and love you give out to the world is mesmerising. Thank you for always being a healthy challenge and making sure I remain focused.

To all the incredibly talented creatives who have formed part of this project. David, your honest feedback and drive to make this story as best as it can be have formed such an important part of the journey over the last few years of my writing. Fatima, your ability to bring my design prompts alive has been amazing. The love and understanding you have shown to this book can be seen in the art that exists in these pages. And to Onur, thank you for bringing all of the above together in the book that exists today.

And lastly, my therapist. As much as I found the answers, you asked the questions. Your kindness, professionalism and extensive knowledge underpins the entirety of my writing, and I am forever thankful for your support in my journey.

Printed in Great Britain
by Amazon